Talks in the Blue

a poem in eighty-one parts

Rudy Kikel

orchard house press
port orchard ~ washington

Talks in the Blue
copyright 2008 by Rudy Kikel
published by Orchard House Press

ISBN 978-1-59092-338-2
0 9 8 7 6 5 4 3 2
First edition January 2009

Cover art by Joe Brainard, Untitled ("The Three Graces"), 1979. Used with permission of the Estate of Joe Brainard and courtesy of the Tibor do Nagy Gallery, New York.

Book design by Blue Artisans Design

All rights reserved, including the right to reproduce this book or portions thereof in any form whatsoever, except in the case of short excerpts for use in reviews of the book. Printed in the United States of America.

For information about film, reprint or other subsidiary rights contact:
legal@orchardhousepress.com

Orchard House Press is an international organization involved in publishing books in all genres, including electronic publications; producing games, toys, videos and audio cassettes as well as producing theatre, film and visual arts events. The house and orchard image is a trademark of Orchard House Press.

Orchard House Press
7419 Ebbert Dr SE
Port Orchard WA 98367
www.Orchard HousePress.com
360-769-7174 ph

Library of Congress Cataloging in Publication data available.

Dedicated to
Richard Howard

Talks in the Blue

a poem in eighty-one parts

Rudy Kikel

Miscellany i/ The Gift

      In the Christmas vacation
during which two of my closest
         friends were away—Danny down
south, Mark out west—I spent mornings

      in the library waiting
for words to come, in the hope of
         jump-starting a new poem. None
did. *I heard your call.* Back at work

      I had what I thought was a
breakdown—breakthrough? *Anybody
         home?* Suddenly you were there.
Initially your message to

      me was painfully precise:
"Die" is what it came down to—or
         was it rising up from some
hell of the spirit that it came?

      *I was just trying to get
your attention—and to accustom
         you to (customize you for)
my register.* You brought me down.

      Medication helped. At least
clonazepam would armor me
         against your assaults. I've stopped
taking it and see that whereas

>   friends and lovers abandon
> one (Sterling goes to New York for
>   a week in March), you I might
> be able to count upon. This
>
>   notebook I keep at my side
> is for my messages and your
>   responses. *Me you always
> have with you. God may not exist—*
>
>   *but the devil is real.* **WELL,
> THIS ISN'T THE FIRST TIME YOU'VE HAD
>   TO REMIND YOURSELF THAT IN
> GERMAN THE WORD "GIFT" MEANS POISON.**

Basic training 1/ Penny wise

  Mitigating the horror
of St. Anne's, with its focus on
  three disciplines I showed no
interest in or proficiency

  for—baseball, basketball, and
football—there was the willingness
  of my mother to write notes
excusing me (on account of

  the cold I seemed always to
have) from gym. And once, long before
  that, in the basement of our
house in Astoria, I put

  on a puppet show I charged
a penny to see. It didn't
  meet the aesthetic needs of
one patron, Ralphy by name, who

  wanted his money back. Which
I refused to give. When with his
  older brother and *his* friends
Ralphy returned to press his claim,

  "I've given my mother the
coin," I told the lot—then argued,
  when she appeared, that the boys
were trying to rob me of a

   penny. She shooed them away.
You let them see your mother do
  your fighting for you, making
unlikely your ever joining

   their gang! **YOUR RELATIONS WITH**
RALPHY WERE NOT SO FRAYED THAT THEY
  KEPT HIM FROM JOINING YOU IN
ANOTHER "PERFORMANCE" OF YOURS—

   "WRESTLING," YOU DUBBED IT—WITH ITS
INTIMATIONS (YOU WERE TEN OR
  ELEVEN) OF THE SPORT YOU
WOULD ONE DAY BE EAGER TO PLAY.

Basic training 2/ Astoria story

      Let's just say that no one in
Mrs. Niedermann's 4th grade class
      (other than the offender
himself) rued the day Mario—

      responsible for keeping
teacher's Melba Toast and tea at
      the ready and for freeing
her shoulders up of her sweater

      at start of the school day, then
returning it to them at its
      end—got his come-uppance: sent
by Mrs. N to suggest that

      the building's heat be turned up,
he returned to class in tow of
      a custodian (let's call
him Vulcan) for having made of

      a suggestion a command.
"Who does Mario think he is?"
      Vulcan asked. That question, class
knew the answer to: teacher's pet,

      who class thought could have done no
wrong—until that day, when in front
      of his classmates Mrs. N
proceeded to dress Mario

down—from that day forward pet
no more. *A cautionary tale
about a woman's guessing
what side her toast was buttered on?*

**HOW SHOULD YOU NOT HAVE AVAILED
YOURSELF OF YOUR MOTHER'S FAVORS
WHEN FROM THE OTHER QUARTERS
OF YOUR LIFE YOU WERE MET—FROM THE**

**ROWDY BOYS ON 42
STREET—BY REVULSION; AND FROM YOUR
FATHER, BY DISAPPOINTMENT,
INCOMPREHENSION AND SILENCE?**

Basic training 3/ Doran Avenue agonistes

      With Georgie "Porgie" in the
role of Mary, and I, my face
        smeared with blood (catsup, that is),
a car accident victim in

      her arms, the door opened on
a Piéta, in the playing
        of a "joke" on my father,
who went so directly into

      crisis mode we had a hard
time proving we were "just kidding."
        *Other than to bring you to
grief, why had Georgie accepted*

      *a role in this test of a
father's love? You hated Georgie,
        he you, your horns locked in the
struggle for the 12-year-old heart*

      *of Janice T. Once he had
spit in the face of your sister
        and made her cry, whom you then
followed home, solicitous it*

      *might have seemed of her feelings,
but really—as you knew and as
        Georgie and the whole street might
have guessed—in your reluctance to*

fight. YOU WOULD HAVE YOUR REVENGE—
AT THE BIRTHDAY PARTY OF YOURS
TO WHICH EVERY KID ON THE
BLOCK HAD BEEN INVITED, JUST NOT

GEORGIE—IN HIS POSTURE OF
A SUPPLICANT TO WHOM YOU WERE
PLEASED TO BE MAGNANIMOUS,
WELCOMING HIM, PUSHING ON HIM

SODA, CAKE AND COOKIES. HOW
MUCH HUMBLING OF HIMSELF HAD IT
TAKEN TO BRING HIM TO YOUR
THRESHOLD, BEGGING TO BE LET IN?

Basic training 4/ Keychain of being

      Tammy C's puberty burst
like a bomb in Glendale, leaving
      the other girls in her dust
and attracting from all over

      town boys on their bicycles
to her row house stoop, which adjoined
      our own, mine and my sister's—
on which we discussed the lucky

      rabbits' feet of different
colors she kept dangling from her
      keychain, as she kept dangling
her string of courtiers, to each

      of which she assigned a foot.
Of course you never knew what shift
      might alter your place in line,
the weekend I went upstate with

      my folks, I went from one to
three (white to green, was it?) in the
      chain, lost ascendancy I
was never able to regain.

      But Tammy's expedient
of maintaining order among
      her suitors may have failed her
the afternoon Butch E wrestled

   her to the ground and felt her
up. Indignant, I ran home to
   ring the doorbell for Tammy's
mother who luckily wasn't

   home. *You might have attempted
to fend Butch off—by inserting
   yourself between the two. But
instead you did what you always*

   did—sought some mother for help.
BRAVOS TO BUTCH E, IN '50S
   **GLENDALE ONE HARBINGER OF
THE DAWN OF SEXUALITY.**

Basic training 5/ The killing fields

       It was Richard C's control
I was under in the eighth grade,
          as he made clear by punching
me every time I passed his desk.

       Once I was about to pass
it by untouched, when my flinching
          in anticipation of
a blow caught him by surprise and

       he remembered to hit me.
Then there was Butch E, who swept through
          Glendale like an invading
Hun, climbing onto Tammy C,

       on her back by the handball
court (and squeezing her breasts), and once,
          with a troop of other boys,
including Andy M, mustered

       around him, onto me (I
was twelve or thirteen) in order
          to pull down my pants. Only
my threat "to tell everyone" he

       was a pervert caused him to
desist. Strange fastidiousness—
          when I was probably the
only "pervert" on the scene. Then

   at a neighborhood rock 'n'
roll party, I tried to save face
   by pretending I did not
believe the beer bottle I had

   just drunk from had been full of
Andy's piss—when of course it had
   been. *Punches, a strip search, "piss"
beer—the Glendale you grew up in*

   meant to wear you down. **OR LACKED
FOR NOTHING AS A BREEDING GROUND
   FOR GAMES OF DOMINANCE AND
SUBMISSION, S/M, EVEN RAUNCH.**

Basic training 6/ The Eddie factor

      Growing pains, Dr. Stern, our
family physician called the
        fits of anxiety which
brought me to him—and which did not

      abate until, in the course
of my washing basement windows
        on our connected Tudor
home, what would become a reason

      to live bicycled by—or
Eddie S did, contact with whom
        produced a template of teen
life I soon adopted as my

      own, specifying a means
of conveyance, the bicycle;
        a part-time job, as a Long
Island Pressboy; travel options,

      to other parts of Brooklyn
and Queens, on the look-out for girls;
        and an abiding pastime,
sitting on the stoops of Glendale

      girls or retiring to "rec"
rooms in which we danced slow numbers,
        lindies and cha chas to the
45s we bought as "seconds,"

   fresh—or wilted—from their first
exposures in juke boxes. But
   had no sex. *Your involvement
in '50s Glendale teen dating*

   *rituals delayed by years
the coming out rituals of
   your own.* **THE TEEN LIFE YOU CHOSE
CAME WITH AN IDENTITY THAT**

   **SEEMED CONSIDERABLE TO
YOU THEN, BEST FRIEND TO EDDIE S,
   WHOM—A RELIGION IT GAVE
TO YOU TOO—YOU FRANKLY ADORED.**

Basic training 7/ Days of 1957

       There was my adoration
of Eddie S and bedroom games
       with Ricky T and Rob L-
so information was coming

       to me about what "turned me
on"—but to construct a lifestyle
       consonant with those feelings...
No, better to live a lie. I

       did what the other boys were
doing, dating girls, but with more
       stoop time with them (I hated
sports) and lindy skills surpassing

       those of any other boy
in Glendale, I seemed provided
       with advantages I was
seen as having abused, tying

       up the affections of girls
and leaving other boys with my
       discards—as their spokesman Bob
D made clear to me on the day

       he threatened to "beat my ass."
If your parents didn't think there
       was anything wrong with your
getting them to fight your battles

        for you, Bob's mother, to whom
your parents appealed, asking her
        to get her son to leave you
alone, was without a doubt. *What*

        did her assurance that no
one would hear of this visit to
        her signify but that there
was something shameful in it for

        you? **TODAY YOU CAN THANK BOB**
FOR HAVING BROUGHT YOU WITH ONE PUNCH
        TO YOUR SENSES—AND OUT OF
A GAME YOUR HEART JUST WASN'T IN.

Basic training 8/ Alvin's example

   When the bottom dropped out of
my Glendale "love life," there living
    on the same block I did was
Alvin T, who had established

   links outside the neighborhood
that I could avail myself of—
    to the Flora Dora, say,
in Jackson Heights, dominated

   by the Flora Dora Girls—
three crones on piano, bass, and
    drums positioned behind the
bar—a three-headed Cerberus

   to whom simply by crossing
its threshold we were, with our youth
    and beauty, throwing sops. *First
in terms of grade-point average*

   *at Sacred Heart, last when it
came to sports, suddenly you were
    good at something again, and
Dangerous*, Alvin sharing with

   you a letter from Jeff, his
lover, forty-five to Alvin's
    seventeen—in which over
and over—as if it were his

doom, a statement of his plight
he was helpless not to inscribe
or move on from—there they were:
the words "I love you." **AND PERHAPS**

**JEFF DID. FRESH FROM GYM CLASSES
IN WHICH ONLY YOUR MOTHER'S NOTES
FORESTALLED YOUR FINDING OUT THAT
NO ONE WANTED TO PLAY WITH YOU,**

**HOW SHOULD YOU NOT HAVE NEEDED
LESSONS IN HOW NOT TO MISUSE
THE POWER TOOLS YOUR YOUTH AND
LOOKS SUDDENLY STUCK IN YOUR HANDS?**

Basic training 9/ Jean Genet moments

"Why do you let them kiss you
like that?" Dennis M said to me
    after watching me one day
in history class getting pecked

    by Dan F and Rocco D.
I didn't know how to answer
    him—I'm a sucker for the
attention? I'm just a boy who

    can't say No? One time I did
say No. Dan had gotten hold of
    my algebra book and crammed
it full of flowers. In a fit

    of pique, I wiped them off on
his jacketed back. I didn't
    want his flowers sticking my
pages together, impeding

    my study. *A pleasant way
to reinterpret those events—
    but, alas, untrue. Dan and
Rocco's fascination with you*

    *took the form of punches; the
flowers you say Dan let rain in
    your algebra book was the
spit he coughed up. Any student*

bully was free to pummel
you at St. Anne's—a Catholic
all-boys' prep school—in the course
of establishing his "manhood"—

that delicately balanced,
perhaps wavering flower then.
THEY WERE PUNCHING YOU SO AS
NOT TO KISS YOU, PRETTY LITTLE

BLOND THAT YOU WERE IN HIGH SCHOOL—
HONORING YOUR ATTRACTIVENESS
IN THE ONLY WAY TO THEM
CULTURALLY PERMITTED THEN.

Two worlds 1/ Fraternity ordeals

        Was I uncovering some
paradigm of class relations
        in Latin America,
in which Tau Alpha Zeta was

        said to take an interest,
or signaling just how far I
        was willing to go to join—
along with Cab V, my best friend

        from high school and secret crush—
the fraternity's chapter at
        St. Anne's? As part of "hazing,"
I had been asked all week to wear

        the tattered garb-torn shirt and
pants, straw hat and red bandana—
        of an "insignificant
half-breed" peasant dog, one who came

        equipped with his own paddle,
inviting use, his underwear
        smelling from broken eggs and
sardines. But those ordeals were as

        nothing compared to the test
of Hell Night, when blindfolded and
        on my knees, I was told by
"kennelmaster" Stanley to drop

my hand into a toilet
bowl and to feed on what I found.
       I picked up something soft and
squishy floating there (afterwards

       discovered to be a peeled
and waterlogged banana), and,
       after a pause, proceeded
to raise it to my mouth—when I

       was told to drop it. *Not the
last time your readiness to eat
       shit would keep a man at your
side.* **ALL FOR LOVE? HEAVEN APPROVES.**

Two worlds 2/ Doppel dating

The story: a double date.
The time: a weekend night. Action:
   my hero picks up first his
best friend, then his steady, then his

   best friend's date (a role which sees
frequent cast changes, in a play
   with only three meaty parts),
knowing that the part of the date

   he most looks forward to is
when it's "over," when the girls have
   been redeposited in
their homes, and my hero and his

   best friend are left talking in
the blue Ford, the friend with whom my
   hero has been long in love.
Suddenly, it occurred to you, my

   hero here, to improvise
new lines for yourself by tearing
   up the rug with Pamela
Morris at a Sacristy Chapel's

   party one night, painfully
ignoring your steady, Mary
   Lou. That left your best friend, Cab,
and Mary Lou to improvise

on their own. They started to
date, got married two years later,
and had a child, and you turned
out to be a lord attendant

to the story's central line
only, a snag in the way of
its resolution—or, worse,
a propmaster—provider of

the required Ford. The role I
would have relished in '62
had not yet been written. **YOUR
BLESSINGS ON CAB AND MARY LOU.**

Two worlds 3/ Recognition scene

*Why should you have been surprised
when in the back room at Pam Pam's,
    gone now, on Third Avenue,
some queen, in order to chat you*

*up, separated himself
from a group that had held you in
    its sights—what was your name? where
were you from?—before dropping one*

*hand into your lap and to
all within earshot reporting
    "Big balls, small cock," as if you
were horse flesh at auction—or a*

*slave—about whom one might have
said "Good teeth, bloody gums"?* What was
    Manhattan gay life but one
big sex bazaar in the '60s,

at which every weapon at
one's disposal was called into
    play and one bettered one's own
chance of scoring by destroying

the competition? *"Yes, but
it's a grower,"* you might have piped
    back—or *"Not that you'll get the
chance to confirm—or deny—that*

*observation"—anything
but let the "bitch" interfere with
 your presentation of self.
But no, your tail folded between*

 your legs, you slunk away! I
wasn't so much struck speechless then
 as lost in amazement that
so much—or so little!—could be

 deduced from so miniscule
a tap. **IN THE WAY OF PLUMBING**
 YOU'VE LACKED FOR NOTHING, AS LONG
EXPERIENCE MUST NOW HAVE PROVED.

Two worlds 4/ Non-recognition scene

        After discovering at
a party (from two men who were
           lovers, Estaban and Tim)
that Patrick H, who attended

        school with me, was gay, he of
the remarkable blue eyes and
           impeccable fraternal
credentials, how I relished talks

        with him—in the blue!—that I
expected to ensue about
           our mutual straddling of
two worlds—college life and gay life—

        and possibly not only
talks... So I was excited to
           see Patrick and Tim sitting
at Pam Pam's. "Who," I asked of Tim,

        "is your cute friend?", whereupon
Patrick laid his head down on his
           hands, which were on the table,
and didn't look up until I

        had passed, like a bad headache,
away. Like a Grand Dame, Patrick
           had chosen not to "know" me.
Back at school, the incident was

      not alluded to; the blue,
impenetrable. *Consider*
      the possibility, will
you, that associating with

      you in the early sixties —
with your lavender brush having
      himself tarred, in Patrick's view —
might then have well amounted to

      the kiss of death at St. Anne's?
WHICH WAS NOT THE WORLD! EYES NOT MET
      MEANT THE FOSTERING OF A
BRAVE NEW COMMUNITY DEFERRED.

Two worlds 5/ Speaking in tongues

      It was Lexi M, St. Anne's
dandy and my then confidant,
      who divulged to Pamela
M the secret of my gayness

      and that of Ronnie B, who
was dating her, leading to the
      presenting of alternate
plans of action apropos of

      Ronnie's future—Pam's straight, mine
gay—while Ronnie sat between us
      at a cafeteria
table drawing pictures of tongues

      hanging from open mouths, like
those of dogs parched or gasping for
      breath, which I took as silent
corroboration of my case

      for his "freedom." *The force of
your presentation would have been
      improved had you not ended
up—at Sam's saloon, where the talks*

      *that evening continued on—
supported by Pam's "motherly"
      arms and fired up about how
much you hated being gay.* **WHAT**

WAS THERE TO CHAMPION ABOUT
THE PERILOUS DOUBLE LIFE YOU
    LED IN '61, WHEN THERE
WAS FOR YOU NO SINGLE ONE? NO

    MATTER. YOU LOST THE BATTLE,
WON THE WAR—FORSAKING LEXI
    (THE ALEXANDRIA YOU
WOULD BE LEAVING! IF IT WASN'T

    HE WHO WAS LEAVING YOU—FOR
GRAD SCHOOL) AND GAINING IN RONNIE
    A TRUSTY COMPANION OF
YOUR LAST LUSTY DAYS IN NEW YORK.

Two worlds 6/ Passing fancies

     It felt all right for me to
orchestrate raids by denizens
        of one "family" I'd worked
my way into—that of the Hay

        Loft in Baldwin, Long Island—
on another, my college life—
        taking for instance to a
fraternity dance Elaine N,

     a lesbian I knew from
the "Loft" who was eager to pose
        for the night as a married
Jewess, the act convincing my

     "brothers" that like Benjamin
with Mrs. Robinson I was
        "getting some"; and not just them,
but all the world, the performance

     continuing with Elaine
stripped of her brassiere and making
        out with me, so as to turn
up the heat in other drivers

     stopped like us at a red light.
Not so smart when the invasion
        occurred in reverse, as on
the night Mangiabello and

*some buddies of his entered
the "Loft", you managing to slip
with luck undetected out
whose college career he could—had*

*he seen you—have crushed like a
bug.* **IN LIEU OF A LATER TIME'S
GUERRILLA THEATER, YOU
WERE PERFORMING "HOUSE OF RUDY"**

**RITUALS, NOT SO MUCH TO
CHANGE THE WAY OF THE WORLD AS TO
AMASS "POINTS" UNTO YOURSELF
FOR A REASSURING "REALNESS."**

Two worlds 7/ Life in the theater

      It wasn't to act on stage
but for a while to stop acting
          (whose college world was a stage)
that I palled around with the one

      gay member I knew of in
the theater group at St. Anne's,
          its Sacristy Stage, only
once appearing in a school play,

      in the role of Ambrose, in
Thornton Wilder's "The Matchmaker,"
          in which, ironically, I
recapitulated the part

      I played in life, suitor to
Kathy D, my Ermengarde—and
          won applause. *How should you have
Presided over the Senior*

      *Class, you thought without a "beard"
at your side? You deferred for years
          the romantic involvements
that would have made* sense *for you—not*

      *to mention how long you kept
Kathy stalled in hers, whom you told
          you had a disclosure to
make* ("I think I know what that is,"

> *she responded) once you'd left*
> *New York for Pennsylvania.* **BUT**
> **NOT SO STALLED THAT YOU'RE NOT (DEAR KATHY) FRIENDS TO THIS DAY. AH, FOR**
>
> **THE INNOCENCE—IGNORANCE!—**
> **OF 'SIXTIES CATHOLIC SCHOOLING,**
> **WHICH ALLOWED YOU FOR YEARS TO**
> **"GO" WITH GIRLS—TO FRATERNITY**
>
> **DANCES, PARTIES AND PROMS, NOT**
> **PETITION THEM FOR SEX AND NOT**
> **HAVE THEM OR ANYONE ELSE**
> **SUGGEST THAT ANYTHING WAS "WRONG."**

Two worlds 8/ Fraternity apocrypha?

    What made me its "best social
chairman," as among some of my
        TAZ brethren I was
reputed to be? The very

    thing that after attending
an all-boy prep school made college
        so welcome—my ease around
girls. And my quest for opposite

    numbers (social chairladies?)
on nearby college campuses—
        chief among them Kings College—
heavily Jewish, hence "easy"—

    and planning with them—on both
sides sight unseen—house parties with
        their sisters and my brothers.
Remember the Kings College bash

    the brothers left en masse, but
not before soaking—baptizing!—
        the basement floor in the house
of one co-ed, voting with their

    penises in support of
a decision that this set of
        sisters, "easy" or not, were
dogs. **NO COMPLAINTS WERE DIRECTED,**

  AS THEY WOULD BE TODAY AND
AS YOU WOULD HAVE BEEN AWARE OF
  THEN, TO THE FRATERNITY
OR THE SCHOOL; YOU WEREN'T AT THE

  PARTY, HAVING IN KATHY
D A BOON COMPANION—SO THE
  TALE MAY BE APOCRYPHAL—
BUT IT'S BEEN ADDED TO THE LORE

  OF TAZ, SUSTAINING
ITS IMAGE OF BEING ST. ANNE'S
  "ANIMAL FRAT." WITH WHICH YOU
WERE HAVING LESS AND LESS TO DO.

Two worlds 9/ Paris is burning

      The snapshot: gold highlights on
a field of green. Apples on the
      leafy tree before which I
stand on my parents' farm: golden;

      hair and pants in shades of gold
that for men had not yet been glimpsed
      on college campuses in
the '60s. (The Carnabie Street

      and San Francisco scenes were
yet to be "made.") And this was the
      photo—sight unseen by Vince
L, the President of your frat—

      you tacked up near the ballot
box in your run for President
      of the Senior Class. "Get it
down," Vince insisted, after it

      was up. *People are taking
one look at it, asking "Who does
      this guy think he is?" "Is he
in love with himself—or what?" and*

      voting for the other guy.
I knew who and what I was, but
      wasn't about to broadcast
my identity when even

      those without a fully charged
decoder—my schoolmates—could be
      so discomfited; as for
being in love with myself—a

      physician would have labeled
me narcissistic—who else knew
      me enough to love me? **HERE
I FANCY YOU AS PARIS WITH**

      **GOLDEN APPLES GALORE TO
BESTOW ON THE HEAVENLY QUEEN
      YOU THOUGHT "MOST FAIR." AND WHY, YOU
WONDERED, MIGHT THAT NOT BE YOURSELF?**

The Remo Elegies 1/ Melissa K

"I address you, Monsieur Le
Baron, on this autumn—tinted
    twilight of the foul-weather
Gods"—so starts a Melissa K

    letter to me, alluding
by its style to—or commenting
    ironically upon-a
High Romantic way of speaking

    we were both picking up from
Dr. Remo I, our St. Anne's
    University teacher
in German 9—and my mentor—

    whose classes—no, whose person—
had unleashed in me a storm (that
    would be a Sturm und Drang) of
poems, plays and stories. Melissa

    and I—under Dr. I's
tutelage—would "make our debuts
    in the Belles-Lettres Monde
as letter stylists," she proposed.

    "More likely fifth-rate scribblers,"
she sensibly added, "in the
    Two-Bit Writing League!" *Who came
to her senses the night you*

*and she visited Dr. I.'s
digs for some "intellectual
   conversation" and the two
of you let her walk herself back*

to her subway stop. **THE MORE
BETWEEN YOU AND DR. I THAN
   INTELLECTUAL CHAT TOOK
ITS OCCASION THAT NIGHT TO GET**

   SAID. When in "The Godfather"
a door shuts Diane Keaton from
   the kissing of her husband's
ring, I think of Melissa K.

The Remo Elegies 2/ The mythmaker

      Shortly after my sharing
with Professor I my first poems,
         he declared me on the same
"plane" as Cavafy, allowing

      as how I was "now bound by
conscience never to renounce [my]
         most sublime impulses to
artistic perfection. *Oh, yes?*

      And your Professor I speaks
in a letter of "placing these
         chemicals" — his own — "on a
mattressed elevation" so that

      "the storm of [his] fatigue" might
be "serened." That is — cutting through
         the florid hyperbole —
he was simply going to bed.

      But was anything simple
once his purple prose was applied
         to it — or even itself?
He was only comfortable

      in the realm of myth and myth-
making and you were his mytho-
         poeic project that year. How
many notches do you have to

>   *ratchet the rhetoric down*
> *before he can be found to have*
>   *said something true about your*
> *work then?* **YOU SUSTAINED FIFTEEN YEARS**
>
> **OF CORRESPONDENCE WITH HIM.**
> **LETTING YOURSELF BELIEVE — ON SOME**
>   **"PLANE" — YOU WERE "HIS ONLY" — BY**
> **HIM — "FAVORED AMONG [HIS] STUDENTS" —**
>
>   **AND WOULD YOU EVER HAVE TURNED**
> **TO POETRY FOR WHAT YOU'VE CALLED**
>   **YOUR LIFE HAD ST. ANNE'S NOT BEEN**
> **SUPPLIED WITH A PROFESSOR I?**

The Remo Elegies 3/ Within arm's reach

      In a letter from the mid-
'60s—I'm guessing—Professor
      I responded to the plaint,
recopied from a letter of

      mine, that sexuality
in my life was becoming an
      "obsession." But sex was a
solution, not a problem, he

      seemed to counsel—"If the life
preserver is within arm's reach,
      why are you screaming at me
to hand it to you?"—but only

      so long, he added, as I
chose not to "wallow" in one of
      the "specifics," sex itself.
And what did Dr. I also

      prescribe but "mastering the
art of duplicity," letting
      society "smile sweetly"
upon you by day, and then by

      night becoming the Other,
a creature consigned to "slither
      in shadows," the pleasures ("Fun,
ain't it?") and pains of which double

life ("little do you know how much pain") you were enduring, you thought, already and seeking an alternative to. **BUT IT**

COULD **BE DONE! WHEN YOU ASKED OF DR. F IF SAPPHO WAS A LESBIAN,** *"YOU* **SAID IT,"** *HE* **QUIPPED. THAT IS, HE WOULD NOT. WHEN THE**

MERE EXISTENCE OF GAYNESS WAS BEING DENIED, DR. I MADE YOU THE GIFT OF A LIFE'S ROAD MAP YOU GREEDILY SURVEYED.

The Remo Elegies 4/ Of two minds

      You would write poems under
your own name, in '67
      you stated. But inasmuch
as "several generations"

      must precede the absorption
of homosexuality
      into the bodies of both
scholarship and Writing itself,

      Dr. I wisely advised
not. *Furthermore, as he pointed out,*
      "homosexuals would for
a long time be ransacking the

      universe, turning every-
thing upside down, their feet moving
      through blood and tears, hands, always
empty, clutching and grasping for

      the beyond, out of reach, in
order to quiet the monster"
      which can be said *"to gnaw at*
their vitals." Anticipations

      of the existence—and of
what might seem to some the methods—
      of Queer Studies?! Consider,
though, how much his gnawing monster

was Dr. I's creation,
who by counseling me to "keep
    the breath of life in [my pen
name R. J.] Stark," consigned me to

    a kind of Jekyll and Hyde
existence—an alternative
    "Stark" indeed. **BUT THAT WAS NOT
HIS LAST WORD: EVIDENCE OF THE**

    **OLD, PRE-STONEWALL GUARD GIVING
ITS RELUCTANT (OR NOT!) NOD TO
    THE NEW, HIS LETTER CONCLUDES
WITH "BLESSINGS" ON YOUR DECISION.**

The Remo Elegies 5/ Sex and spirit

The "fondling" rather gives it
away: a letter from you—"a
jewel sparkling in sunlight"—
he promised he would "fondle," so

as "to absorb its glitter."
Forget the High Romantic gloss
he put on things: Dr. I.
wanted to get into your pants.

One letter even has him
imagining orgasm with you—
as "an ecstasy of shoot-
ing stars shrieking through space." Of course

that was only after I
had bragged to him about having
become a "much sought-after
fucker," which places the letter

after my role-transforming
Paris summer of '66.
And, in fact, in Dr. I's
view, body and spirit didn't

undergo their accustomed
divorce (another letter he
described as "the wedding of
perfect orgasm: salvation"), and

sex, like art or mysticism,
was a means of achieving
"union with the Divine, though
conditions are," he allowed, "in

homosexual sex, more
difficult." **THE MORE IMPRESSIVE**
 THE LOVE YOU TWO SHARED, IN WHICH
A MAN'S SPIRIT WAS "FILLED WITH THE

 BEAUTY OF JOYFUL SADNESS"
SIMPLY BY THOUGHTS OF HIS "SPARKLING"—
 "THIS IS YOUR ESSENCE," DR.
I DECLARED—HIS "BEAUTIFUL BOY."

The Remo Elegies 6/ In the name of God

      You'd think I would have learned my
lesson! There I was—fresh from my
        ecstatic—sentimental!—
summer of '66 viewing

      of "Jedermann" on the steps
of the Cathedral in Salzburg—
        attesting—babbling—as to
how I had never before been

      "so able to give myself
over" to Dr. I.'s "God." "Kneel
        before me," he shot back, "and
beg my forgiveness for thinking

      I have come *through belief* to
my conception of God." But, no,
        in '69 I asked him
to pray for me, only to be

      told he could not—he was not
a child anymore, "nursery
        theology" being his
name for the "legalisms" he felt

      required to spout at St. Anne's.
*You looked for theological
        certainties from Dr. I—
and he would not even yield you*

      epistemological
ones: "We don't know reality,"
      he mused, "but intuit it."
DR. I WAS A CATHOLIC

    "WITH MUCH OF THE FRINGE TRIMMED OFF"—
AND, IN FACT, INASMUCH AS HE
    BELIEVED ONLY THOSE WHO LOST
THEMSELVES COULD "FIND GOD," HE WAS MORE

    INTERESTED ALWAYS IN
WHAT RESULTED FROM THE TRIMMING
    DOWN OF CERTAINTIES THAN IN
FAITH ITSELF—EVEN FAITH IN HIM.

> *Dr. Remo J. Iannucci, a former language professor ... was found dead in his home at East 86th Street in Manhattan on Sunday [June 3]. He was 65.*
>   *Dr. Iannucci, a specialist in medieval German literature... retired this spring.*
>   —The New York Times, June 6, 1979

The Remo Elegies 7/ Fire and ice

"When the fitful fever of
life flickers out"—so ran Dr.
    I's envisioning of his
own death—"I shall be led On High

    by the Seraphims' trumpets'
sweet-sounding song to Eternal
    Springtime where my soul will be
frozen forever in the fire

    of cosmic Consciousness." Which
passage was followed by one of
    his *Stimmungsbrechungen*: "Whew!
out-romantic me on *that* if

    you can," as if anyone
was competing! *"Found dead in his
    home,"* the New York Times obit
reads. Of the black rubber mat spread

    on Dr. I's living room
floor and the ashtrays with butts from
    two kinds of cigarettes in
them (of whose existence a great

*friend of Dr. I's of the
period assures me) there was
     no mention.* ALLOWING, AS
DR. I DID, THAT IN ORGASM

     MINDS MAY BE FREE TO UNITE
WITH THE DIVINE, WHO DENIES THE
     POSSIBILITY THAT IN
HIS LAST SUCH MOMENT—"EMBITTERED"

     ON ACCOUNT OF BEING IN
THE SPRING RELIEVED OF HIS TEACHING
     POSITION—THE ONE TRUE LOVE
OF HIS LIFE—AND WITH WHAT AHEAD

     BUT AN IMPENDING MOVE TO
PITTSBURGH—HE DECIDED HE WOULD
     SIMPLY NOT COME BACK? THERE WOULD
THIS TIME BE NO STIMMUNGSBRECHUNG.

The Remo Elegies 8/ Do I wake or sleep?

       He would profess ignorance
of what he was going to say;
       then, afterwards, wonderment
("whither has my mind gone? whither

       arrived?"), as if he might need
one day to attribute to "spells"
       of "automatic writing"
the passages in his letters

       to me—from a single line
to as many as five pages—
       he would copy directly
from Volume Two (1910 to

       '26) of the letters
of Rilke published by Norton.
       Plagiarism on the part of
a college professor—and this

       was the charlatan, letters
from whom helped you plot the course of
       your life! Passages were so
beautiful, a long excerpt from

       one to Rudolph Bodländer,
for instance, amounting to a
       profound meditation on
the church's failure to come to

        terms with human love. And how
precise his choices were—always
        the passage apposite to
a then current quandary of

        mine, never the same one twice.
NOW YOU ARE ENTERING INTO
        THE SPIRIT OF DR. I'S
ELABORATE WIZARDRY, THOUGH

        IN THE END THE JOKE MAY HAVE
BEEN ON HIM, WITH EACH CRIBBED PASSAGE
        CONSTRUCTING A FACADE THAT
INURED HIMSELF FROM BEING KNOWN.

The Remo Elegies 9/ Stargazing

      His surviving "the pain" of
his "deep loneliness," he told you
      repeatedly, depended
on your keeping in touch with him.

      But you couldn't perform that
simple task! "Shortly after you
      stopped writing to him, Dr.
I died," Dr. H told you, "of

      a heart attack." Unless it
was a broken heart! On the day,
      years after graduation
from St. Anne's, he presented me—

      to a class of his I was
visiting—as an art star, I
      felt I distressed him by
failing to wax oracular.

      Limiting information
coming to him might have made sense
      then... those school breaks he begged off
seeing me—which only tended

      to topple my pedestal.
MAY NOT THE "SURVIVAL" DR.
      I DISCOVERED FOR HIMSELF
HAVE BEEN INSPIRED BY NOT RILKE

       BUT HOLDERLIN ? "FEEL WITH ME,"
DR. I ASKED, "THE LUSCIOUS LOVE
        OF LONELINESS CREATING
GODS SO DETACHED FROM ALL THAT IS

       NATURAL AND COMING TO
REST IN THE SERENITY OF
        ONE'S OWN OLYMPUS." NO PAIN
OBTAINED TO LONELINESS ONCE ONE

       WAS PROVIDED COMPANY
CUT OFF FROM THE WORLD, AND IN THAT
        PROJECT WHO YOU REALLY WERE
WOULD HAVE BECOME IRRELEVANT.

Away 1/ Mr. Charisma

      He had a zillion pearly
whites, as were evident in the
          headshot of himself he claimed
had been used in a toothpaste ad;

      that smile apparently held
its attraction for Monacan
          Queen Grace Kelly, too, coming
across him in the South of France

      who bade him sit beside her
and tell her all about himself.
          Power over people—that's
the tool he lay claim to: for the

      three-car pile-up blocks from the
apartment we shared, Maxim had
          an explanation: so struck
were the drivers by the sight of

      his legs in his summer shorts
that they lost control of their cars.
          Everyone seemed a fan, just
not yourself. Why not? *On account*

      of his posture—no, posing—
one foot up on the library
          steps, his basket displayed to
advantage **(HE WAS BIG, GIVE HIM**

THAT) *at a meeting for a
first date, whereon you recognized
 a narcissism as avid,
as needy, and as unavowed*

*as your own. Which didn't stop
your hooking up with him as his
 lover for two years.* **YOUR FIRST
TIME LIVING AWAY FROM HOME, YOUR**

**CHECK LIST HAD A MEASLY TWO
ITEMS ON IT: GET DIGS OF YOUR
 OWN AND FIND A MAN. EVEN
LIKING HIM WAS NOT ON YOUR LIST.**

Away 2/ The literary life

       In each class I took with him,
Dr. J would spout large chunks of
       Shakespeare, but Maxim was the
only member of my peer group

       at State College who seemed to
live by and breathe literature.
       When I met him in grad school
he had already established

       "dialogues" with dead white men
Shakespeare, Wordsworth, Keats & Shelley;
       in our time together he
added to the pack Henry James

       and Wallace Stevens. "Maxim
on Wordsworth" was so persuasive
       that I felt I needed to
run it by Dr. C, whose class

       in the Lake Poets I was
taking. Corroborated by
       Dr. C: Maxim's reading—
but not to the exclusion of

       mine or, indeed, Dr. C's
own. *Maxim wasn't happy for*
       you in the early '60s
when decidedly queer poems

of yours started appearing
in One magazine. Was your work
not good enough for him when
measured against the classics—who

were becoming, remember,
one by one, his familiars?

Duh! **SACRED MONSTERS THE FRENCH CALL WRITERS, SO RUTHLESS CAN THE**

RESPONSE BE TO WRITING NOT THEIR OWN. DID ANY PLACE MAXIM PARKED HIS PONY PEGASUS IN HAVE TO BE A ONE-MUSE TOWN?

Away 3/ To tell the truth

   They were nice people. So
the curtains came down, the lights up,
    on my realization
of how ill-cast his family,

   met upon graduation,
were for roles Maxim had scripted
    for them in his "Saga of
Violated Love," which fable

   called into question as well
the existence of half-brothers
    every out-of-my-earshot talk
with a gas station attendant

   seemed to conjure up in the
course of our island "honeymoon."
    As for getting a B-plus,
not an A, during the summer

   session I was away, his
story involved rewriting from
    memory a term paper,
in the wake of a basement flood

   that took his original
essay and all his notes but left
    no signature of itself
on baseboard, furniture or wall.

*Confronted with your disbe-
lief, Maxim came up with a last
      tirade: they weren't lies — the
tale of his car-crashing calves, et*

    *al., but instances of his
Romantic Imagination
    at work. Keats must be rolling
in his Roman grave!* **OR CHEERING**

**   AN INVENTIVENESS THAT YEARS
LATER IN THE FOUNDING OF AN
    URBAN POETRY HOME WOULD
BE FELT AS HIS CREATIVE BREATH!**

Away 4/ Having words

  A nice example of a
"silly queen," which one of his friends
   had called me—or so Maxim
dutifully—or not!—reported,

  I seemed privileged (spoiled?) to
him; he, product of the Lower
   East Side, angry to me—which
added fire to our discussions

  of "Look Back in Anger," "The
Blacks," anything by Amiri
   Baraka. Those points of view
collapsed into each other, though,

  fostering a depthlessness—
an ignorance of each other—
   or a brisk clearing of the
air—when after a long, boozy,

  and argumentative night,
I ended up surprising both
   of us by unfurling at
Maxim the 'N' word, in whose train

  the 'R' word followed. Whereat
Maxim was all smiles. He hadn't
   without such awareness been
happy; could I be happy *with*

  it? *Maxim gave you a boxed*
set of "The Greek Tragedies" at
  parting—and what but Agon-
cum-Anagnorisis had you

  both come through? But you... so small,
unforgiving and vulgar had
  you become, you gave him two
hundred lousy bucks. **SETTING FOOT**

  ON THE SHORES OF SELF-KNOWLEDGE,
THE DIFFERENCES BETWEEN YOU
  LOOMED SO LARGE, YOU TURNED YOUR BOAT
AROUT AND HEADED BACK TO SEA.

Away 5/ No room at the inn

       I'd come to Paris in the
summer of '66, it seemed,
          to take to my bed in the
company of girls (mostly) from

       the University of
Kansas; when it was discovered
          the pension had promised
to provide one more bed than it

       had available, the girls
maintaining their integrity—
          or forced to have it maintained
for them—it fell to me to be

       stabled across the street in
the Hotel Printemps, even as
          supper continued to be
provided au pension. *Quite*

       the Scheherazade you proved—
the implication being that
          you, anyway, were not in
Kansas anymore—in your tales,

       for instance, of how Alain,
concierge and your tour guide to
          its "underworld"—would, having
detected no obvious "mess"

among them, make up the beds
in the hourly rentals (with which
    the hotel chiefly made its
money) by means of a twelve-inch

    ruler, applying fold marks
to used sheet and pillow cases
    and giving them at least the
look of "freshness." **WHERE BETTER TO**

BEGIN THE REMAKING OF
YOUR LOVE LIFE, WHICH BECAME FOR YOU
    THE SUMMER'S ENDEAVOR, THAN
IN A HOUSE OF LOVE, WHERE YOU WERE?

Away 6/ Greek practicum

      At my welcoming
party to the Hotel Printemps, Alain
      and 'Tilda took turns sitting
in my lap in search of answers

      to the questions hovering
like smoke in the air: what was I?
      And just as important: what
did I like doing? I knew what

      I wanted to like doing,
though I could count on the fingers
      of one... finger (Nick C, the
Hayloft), the time I had risen

      to the occasion; and here
were Viktor, Denis, Alexandre—
      let's just refer to them by
the composite Paris—rolling

      onto his belly, his butt
wriggling in the air, beckoning
      delightfully. *Normally
I should have been responsible*

      *for corralling opinion
about your not being a real
      man, but a sissy faggot,
and so shutting you down, but now*

the Voice of Paris was too
strong. America, translated
into French as Power, had
only to look himself to top

a frog. **DAY TWO: YOU RUSHED OUT
TO BUY IN A MEN'S BOUTIQUE THE
DUNGAREE JACKET TO GO
WITH THE JEANS YOU AT LEAST HAD THE**

**FORESIGHT TO PACK, COMPLETING
YOUR IMPRESSION OF A COWBOY,
AMERICAN; THE LEFT BANK
MODEL, SUMMER OF '66.**

Away 7/ Tutelary spirit

      In Guy a big brother; in
Alain and Anita "sisters";
      in Viktor the "sibling" most
available for "incest" and

      regrets; even in Irma
a Dark, forbidding Mother, the
      Cerberus at the Hotel
Printemps desk who refused entry

      to the friends—okay, tricks—I
tried sneaking by her. (Over and
      above my summer rental
fee, offering to pay her for

      the hours I had company
might have constituted that all
      important sop.) Then I had
no need of my room afternoons

      anymore. I'd taken up
with Albert R, and his friends Jon
      Jack and Karl-Franz let us have
their digs to romp in afternoons.

      Nothing made so evident
the financial differences
      between you and your "chosen"
French family as—bag in hand

of French pastries your housemates
couldn't have afforded on their
    own—your blowing in on the
hotel kitchen supper (one course

    only: gruel of the day).
It was as if you'd uttered the
    line falsely attributed,
suggests Will Durant, to Marie

    Antoinette: "Let them eat cake."
THE FAMILY AS A LAUNCHING
    PAD YOU'D APPRECIATED
ALWAYS, JUST NOT ITS BINDING TIES.

Away 8/ What I didn't do for love

  My need of another tongue
landed me at the Alliance
   Français where students from all
over the world were asked to give

  up in class speaking a word
of their first. *After a week I
  was offered a berth on the
fast train to facility in*

  French. But that would have meant class
time in the afternoons as well
  as the mornings—and you'd just
fathomed the Piscine Deligny,

  a floating pool on the Seine—
as a result of which you might
  fail your French reading exam
back in Cambridge. **SMALL PRICE TO PAY**

  **FOR MEETING ALBERT R, WITH
WHOM BY AUGUST YOU WERE HOOKED UP.**
  He knew no English, neither
of us any French ... to speak of;

  we still hoped to make a go
of it in Paris, a city
  we believed was the only
one possible "für uns sich

lieben etwas zusammen
aufzubauen." To that end I
   got myself a job teaching
English in a Paris suburb.

   Albert was to join me in
December, his camera classes
      concluded. *Instead doubts crept
in, you flew back to Boston, you*

      stopped answering his letters.
Years flew by... **WHAT WOULD YOU NOT GIVE**
      NOW FOR WORD OF "IMMER DEIN
KLEINER TRAURIGER FREUND ALBERT"?

Away 9/ Die Rechnung, bitte

  My returning to the States
gave Albert the experience,
  he says—the ground giving out
from under him—of falling "in

  einer diefen Abgrund," from
which he issued distress signals
  (will our affair have been for
me just another adventure?),

  commands (my love belongs to
him—don't let another have it),
  and threats: if you don't love me,
I'll lose my mind and take my life.

  His mother in Hamburg keeps
asking what's wrong with him, he takes
  to his bed, suffering from
angina, pleurisy, he can't

  work, needs to work—his mother
wasn't putting him through school, he'd
  lied, she died three years ago—
would I send him a number of

  German Marks? *Amounting to
thirty lousy bucks! But there it
  was—you were American—
by definition rich: pay now*

*and be ready to pay and
pay again.* **IN THE STATES YOU WERE
REAPING BENEFITS FROM THE
BOOK OF YOUR LIFE ALBERT HAD SCHOOLED

YOU IN — CALL IT "PART 2: THE
DEVIL'S SWEET MEATS." ALBERT'S LETTERS —
WHAT BEFELL THEM BUT TO GIVE
EVIDENCE IN THE COURT OF YOUR

MOTHER'S OPINION — AS PROOF
THAT YOU HAD AN EMOTIONAL
LIFE SEPARATE FROM HERS? THAT
YOU FOR ONE HAD GOTTEN AWAY.**

Group 1/ Beating the bush

      The nation had seen the black
and women's movements. Now it was
         our turn. First off, the sleepy
Homophile Union of Boston

      was confronted with the charge,
from its young "firebrands" Stan T. and
         myself among others, that
it wasn't "radical" enough.

      Outside Filene's I handed
out "gay lib" flyers, attended
         Cambridge Common "love-ins," joined
discussion groups. *Liberation*

      language validated a
choice you'd already effected:
         by staying in graduate
school as long as you were able—

      thanks to a deferment that
sent poor working-class kids in your
         stead into the Viet Nam
bush—you avoided trucking with

      "The Establishment." *So much*
for not "making war"; and "love" you
         could hardly have made more of,
in the free time your light class loads

allowed, in the Boston *bush.*
My finest hour came of speaking
    before a subcommittee
at the State House considering

   the granting of civil rights
to gays. There were sixteen of us
    and no opposition—wha'
happened?! **IT WAS ONLY WHEN CHANGE**

   THREATENED THAT THE OTHER SIDE
APPEARED. YOU COULD HAVE PREDICTED
    THE BILL'S FAILURE TO PASS BY
THOSE EMPTY OPPOSITION AISLES.

Group 2/ Southern charm

      In the battle terms by which
they were served up in the '50s,
      sports were anathema to
me, the pain of sitting out gym

      class, unchosen for a game
of table tennis, much less one
      of baseball or basketball,
exquisite. "Liberation" changed

      that, allowing the healing
of our bruised, non-athletic selves
      to begin—in the form of
gay men playing football on the

      banks of the Charles, "taking back
the field," we said, the way women
      were resolving "to take back
the night." *I don't remember the*

      games, only that I scored in
attracting to my side Eddie
      S, the darling of Gay Lib
in Boston, as—decades before

      the term was in general
use—my "trophy wife." Turns out
      Eddie was passing around
that trophy—himself!—and acting

>   *as a "wife" for such other*
> *members of the team as he deemed*
>   *fit (a priest, a writer, an*
> *architect) "in the pursuit of*
>
>   *[his] education." You got*
> *an education too—in the*
>   *duplicity Southern boys*
> *are capable of.* **EDDIE CLAIMED**
>
>   **THAT EVEN THOUGH YOU HAD NOT**
> **WANTED TO HEAR HIM TELL THE TRUTH—**
>   **IT WAS TO PROTECT YOU THAT**
> **HE LIED—HE ALWAYS THOUGHT YOU KNEW.**

Group 3/ Age of Aquarius

      Michael H. amounted to
my very own production of
      "Hair," ushering in an Age
of Aquarius, except in

      reverse: he came back from Nam
and *then* proceeded to "drop out"
      and grow his long, beautiful
hair: an auburn afro. We got

      entangled in each other,
certainly, and not just in his
      hair, becoming in the sack
not two but one palpitating

      entity—Ouroboros
created by the curling of
      our bodies on each other—
head to tail—for which transcendent

      experience we drew on
the assistance of my silver-
      gowned, bedside vial of "Amy"—
raising the question of whether

      we were high on each other
or on her. *After all Michael*
      did for you, nursing you through
your stint of hepatitis, you

> "severed the circle" merely
upon the discovery that he
> had smoked some grass before a
screening and later couldn't talk

> about the film. **DUTIFULLY,
MICHAEL REPORTED EROTIC
> PROPOSALS FRIENDS OF YOURS MADE
TO HIM: DIDN'T THAT INDICATE

> BOTH—IN HIS EFFORT TO MAKE
YOU JEALOUS—THE SLIMNESS OF THE
> HOLD HE MUST HAVE THOUGHT HE HAD
ON YOU AND HIS OWN WANDERLUST?**

Group 4/ Needing help

      The professor at Norfolk
University who hired me
      slipped me, in a brown paper
bag, just as I was about to

      teach a class, obscene poems
by Lord Rochester. The message—
      "Keep your sexuality
under wraps, as I am keeping

      mine"—was clear. So when in class
I was asked, "They're queer, aren't they—
      Vladimir and Estragon?"—
I spouted some '60s strictures

      about the language it was
"politically correct" to use,
      instead of "coming out"—and
hoped my blushing wasn't giving

      me away. Years later I
asked a man I met in a gay
      bar who had been a student
of mine what—when I would discuss

      homosexuality
in reference to Shakespeare, say, or
      Lord Byron—I looked like. "You
blushed a lot," he said. *There was much*

*to blush about! The classes
you had to prepare—wouldn't they
be interfering with your
nightly trolling for tricks on the*

Esplanade? **EARLY GAY LIB
SKIRMISHES MAY HAVE DISCOVERED
WEAKNESSES AMONG SOME OF
ITS RANKS, SO RUNNING PARALLEL**

**TO POLITICS THERE WOULD GROW
THIS NEED OF PEOPLE TO CLEAN THEIR
HOUSES. YOU WOULDN'T JUST YET
BE RELIEVED OF YOUR COMMISSION.**

Group 5/ That shrinking feeling

    I took accounts of my late-
night meanderings on Boston's
        Charles River Esplanade to
a university mental

    health triage nurse who, at my
brandishing like a sword poems
        by Shelley, ridiculed my
defense of sexual "freedom";

    then on to a doctor who,
offering me the option of
        "joining the mainstream," sent me
to Dr. Cant, who, seeing my

    "uncontrollable acting
out behavior" as a mask for
        my despair at not being
straight, invited me to join him,

    his co-therapist (female),
and a group of men like myself,
        seeking "a choice." *Joining the
mainstream—yes, but at the cost of*

    *the diversity you could
be said to bring to it! And "choice"—
        what did that mean but dropping
an identity you'd fought long*

and hard for over the years?
Then how did you square your Gay Lib
　　credentials with therapy
so clearly homophobic? "TELL

ME ABOUT YOUR FATHER," CANT
ASKED IN YOUR FIRST SESSION WITH HIM.
　　"WELL, FIRST OF ALL," YOU ANSWERED,
"HE'S DUMB!", TO WHICH THE GOOD DOCTOR

　　MADE A REMARK THAT ALL YOUR
WORK WITH HIM COULD BE SAID TO BE
　　SIMPLY A GLOSS UPON: "SO
YOU SEE HIM THROUGH YOUR MOTHER'S EYES."

Group 6/ Assisted loving

       To give the disciple his
due, Dr. Cant—an acolyte
       of the then notorious
Irwin Bieber—had halted his

       practice of "shocking" people
into "normality"—for talk
       therapy. Having been "failed"
by the model before, we were

       provided with a "father"
with whom we could talk, the doctor;
       a co-therapist "mother";
and ten "brothers," a surrogate

       family working with whom
we could find support for storming
       the straight and narrow, so if
I reported having had sex

       three times that week with men I
did not know (the group looking bored
       or uneasy) and gotten
a smile from a girl in one of

       my classes, the "family"
would ask me to "tell [them] about
       the girl." *Which goes to show that
talk can be just as coercive*

as that old shock therapy.
Then with all the emphasis on
    getting you to go straight, there
was no address of your drugging,

    drinking and other problems.
ONE THING OF VALUE YOU TOOK FROM
    THE GROUP WAS A NEWCOMER'S
FIRST ADDRESS—A "BOY" ANNOUNCING

    THAT "THE EMPEROR" HAD ON
NO CLOTHES: YOU SOUNDED, HE SAID, "LIKE
    A CHICKEN WITH ITS HEAD CUT
OFF." CONFIRMING SMILES ALL AROUND.

Group 7/ Game

    I needed a woman to
practice my moves upon in the
        game of Normalcy I was
coaxed into playing, and presto!

    there, teaching beside me at
Norfolk University was
        Eleanor R, who seemed to
come replete with a whole set of

    powerful women friends and
the less clearly defined men who
        danced attendance upon them,
as did on his wife Alisson,

    my friend Andy A., to whom
that Christmas I dutifully
        lied about my "progress" at
having gotten with Eleanor

    *"in but not off." Eleanor
was practicing moves on you too,
        crafting you into the man
she would want. From her squeezings of*

    *your hand during the films you
saw with her, you knew precisely
        what she was feeling. Question:
were your own feelings about the*

films registering? **SHE WAS
WILLING TO ALLOW WHAT WITH HER
      YOU WERE NOT — THAT YOU REALLY
WERE HOMOSEXUAL — THOUGH YOU**

**   MUST HAVE ASKED IT OF YOURSELF,
AS (WIPING OUT IN THE PROCESS
      MANY OF YOUR "GAINS" IN THE
GAME) YOUR ONE-NIGHTER IN NEW YORK'S**

**   CLUB BATHS THAT YEAR SUGGESTED,
WHERE YOU APOLOGIZED TO THE
      MEN YOU "ACTED OUT" UPON
FOR HAVING "USED THEM AS OBJECTS."**

Group 8/ Sandy's turn

      Come Tuesdays, some ten of us
would find the group's co-therapist,
      Sandy, available for
projections onto, as mother,

      sister, sweetheart, virgin, whore
(I referred in group to women
      once as "gashes"; "talk about
that," Cant eagerly responded).

      I remember balling when
Sandy's participation in
      group was at an end—the last
in a chain of events prompted

      by Eleanor's espying
the two of them—Cant and Sandy—
      holding hands in Harvard Square
and rushing to tell me—and through

      me the group—what she'd espied.
About Eleanor's coming to
      me with the story, how did
I feel, Dr. Cant wanted to

      know. *How you all felt: bereft—*
to the degree that you had let
      yourselves fantasize about
her. Rivalry with each other,

> *since you were all — in being*
gay — at the same "disadvantage,"
> *you could bear; rivalry with*
Cant, the only "man" in the room

> *whose heterosexual*
credentials were impeccable,
> *you could not.* **OR SO YOU THOUGHT.**
IN ANY CASE, GIVE ELEANOR

> **CREDIT FOR BRINGING TO THE**
TABLE AS NOTHING ELSE HAD HOW
> **YOU EACH FELT ABOUT LOSING**
TO YOUR FATHER YOUR MOTHER'S LOVE.

Group 9/ Mother loving

     "Did she (my mother) like *her*
mother (Nettie)?" Eleanor had
     asked of her on a visit
to my family home. Sending

     her daughters out of Gottschee
to make their ways in the New World
     at sixteen; the letters to
my mother burned along with her

     complaints that her daughters had
never done enough for her—sure,
     there was much about Nettie
to complain of, if one were so

     inclined. My mother was not.
Open that can of worms and what
     question might yet slither out
of it: did I (her son) like his

     mother? *"Too much—not enough?—*
to have another "mother" in
     my life!," as you mused in the
journal of yours beside the bed

     that, in your Charles Street digs for
a nap, Eleanor put her hands
     upon. *She was furious*
with you, as you dutifully

*reported to the group. One
question only Dr. Cant was
interested in putting
to you: what did you feel about*

her reading your journal? **BY
THAT POINT THE SUPPORTS OF YOURS SHE
MIGHT HAVE EXPECTED TO BE
WITH HER—YOUR MOTHER, DOCTOR, AND

GROUP—WERE MARSHALLED AGAINST HER.
YOU LET YOURSELF BE DRAWN TO SHORE.
WITHOUT YOUR BEING A PART
OF IT, "THE MAINSTREAM" RUMBLED ON.**

Miscellany ii/ Termination plans

   For me to "terminate" with
the group and Dr. Cant's blessings
    intact (bringing to an end
my four years' work in group—not just

   dropping out of it) one thing
seemed needful: a demonstrated
    capacity to "have a
relationship," with a woman

   or a man—so scaled down had
the group's checklist become; so scaled
    down, indeed, had my own, the
night I met Craig R in Sporter's.

   A desire like your own you
thought you discovered in him an
    evening later, when finding
you again at Sporter's, Craig grabbed

   you by the elbow, steered you
into the street and home. Here was
    your man: What had his muscling
you out of the bar argued for

   but how much love he had for
you? In short order, his checklist
    expanded (that was love too):
now he wanted to be at your

side always, even though you had a job and he did not. And he wanted you anally receptive to him. Dr. Cant

offered counsel. **NOT BEING FUCKABLE WAS BAD FORM, BUT NOT A MEDICAL CONDITION. AND DID YOU WANT A DOCTOR WHOSE**

WORK HAD BEEN IN THE FIELD OF HELPING GAY MEN "RECOVER" FROM BEING GAY CLEARING THE WAY TO YOUR BECOMING A BOTTOM?

Hot spots 1/ My anima

      In the period between
my playing with cut-outs and my
          collecting of male physique
magazines, I came under *Her*

          sway: once my parents were out
of an evening, leaving at home
          my sister Joan, one year my
junior, and me, I would be drawn

          to their bedroom, where I would
be swathed in a bedsheet, have my
          mother's bedspread thrown over
my shoulder—two ends of which would

          be joined by a jeweled pin—
and presto! there apparent in
          my parents' bedroom mirror,
She was—a lady, a princess,

          a queen, Madonna in
white, who then treated (who else was
          there to see Her?) my sister
to a night of prancing (flashing?)

          about the house that ended
with my parents' return, when all
          trace of Her would have disappeared—
except for once when the living

   room was found littered with shreds
of chenille I had to vacuum
   up. Still, no one except for
myself seemed to think I had done

   anything "wrong." *But wrong it
was—if only on account of*
   the havoc your transvestite
antics might have been making of

   Joan's emotional life! **YOU
HAD NOT VOLUNTEERED NOR WERE YOU
   CALLED AT THE AGE OF NINE OR
TEN TO BE YOUR SISTER'S KEEPER.**

Hot spots 2/ Tommy S

Along with his long whiplash
of a tongue, accommodation
    was his strong suit: once you got
him to attend a peepshow where,

    while you regaled him at the
one end—it hardly mattered which—
    he presented himself at
the other... to drifters by; then

    he got right back to business,
having flushed with water the eye
    you spilled amyl nitrate
into, in a clumsy effort

    to share with him your drugs
while sitting upon his face. Yet
    when his mother and chief care-
taker could not (would not?) be told

    the nature of his disease,
you never thought to visit him,
    your faithfulness being then
to a location (Sporter's) and

    a winnowing process (last
call) and not a person. "Look at
    yourself,"—advised one friend of
Tommy's I'd just turned down. I stared

    in a mirror. I still *looked*
good; I was "free" not to work or
    love, and to spend every night
in a bar—what was he going

    on about? **WHEN THE AIDS QUILT**
CAME TO BOSTON, A PART OF IT
    INVITING INSCRIPTIONS, YOU
ADDRESSED TO HIM A COMPLIMENT

    BEFITTING THE LEVEL OF
INTIMACY THE TWO OF YOU
    HAD ATTAINED. "TO TOMMY," YOU
WROTE, "WHO GAVE THE BEST HEAD IN TOWN…"

Hot spots 3/ An afternoon delight

      I had assigned myself to
toilet detail in the middle
         stall of the first-floor men's room
at Lamont, during exams, when

      the queens' "business" was thought to
improve, freshmen needing relief,
         so the thinking ran, from long
hours of bending over their books.

      Of a sudden, at the tap
of my foot to the newcomer
         to my left, I heard his stall
door slam open and shut and an

      insistent knock on my own.
When I opened it, there he stood—
         his legs spread, shirt yanked up, shorts
pulled to below his balls, cock hard

      and at the ready—the son
of a famous sports figure, a
         dream come true—while to him, as
his sneer instructed me, I was

      anybody, nobody,
a convenience, merely... *In short*
         everything you discovered
you secretly aspired to be

*in an aristocracy
you despaired of joining—here was
someone whose scornful disgust
of your ministrations—even*

*as he availed himself of
them—mirrored your own self-loathing!*
**YOU ONLY ENDED LAMONT'S
TYRANNY OVER YOU BY A**

**MOVE TO BEACON HILL, WHERE AT
SPORTER'S YOU MET MEN WITH WHOM YOU
COULD BOTH FUCK AND TALK. OF COURSE
THAT'S WHEN YOUR DRINKING PICKED UP TOO.**

Hot spots 4/ The Glory Hole Club

A glimpse of yourself in the
early '80s can be discerned
    in the comment of the club
Cerberus, who after testing

    your chops, as it were, on and
for himself, you heard
    say of you to a friend, "There's
a squirrel who's lost his tree," so

    desperate, scurrying from
hole in the wall to hole in the
    wall—in your quest of nuts?—did
you appear, when there was no real

    sustenance there to be had.
Ah, but one could sometimes stumble
    over a porn star of the
stature even of "Al Parker"—

    whose visits and dimensions
were the stuff of urban legends—
    contact with whom would have been
prefaced with libations at one

    of two flanking chapels of
lust—the Eagle, a leather bar,
    and the Spike, for uniformed
men; I found myself so favored

>on the night I saw to the
needs of the Target cover man
>whom I recognized as the
"fireman" in volume 2, number

>1 of Meat magazine, which
I have in my possession to
>this day. **THERE WAS NO GETTING
AWAY FROM IT: WHERE ALL AROUND**

>**SUPPLICANTS STOOD, HOSES IN
HAND, IT WAS TO YOU HE TURNED—O
GREAT DISTINCTION—IF ONLY
FOR THE NONCE—TO PUT HIS FIRE OUT.**

Hot spots 5/ The Mineshaft

  Tableaux vivantes that were a
cross between a Horrow Show and
   Hieronymous Bosch. See here,
propped up on the bar: the "Frozen

  Colonic"—ice man making
his deliveries, cube by cube,
   into another's service
entry—to put some nether fire

  out? And here: "The Swallower"—
in which a man's arm is buried
   in someone's rump up to the
shoulder! Presto—the arm's revealed

  upon extrusion to be
not an arm but a stump. And here:
   "Three Men in Their Tubs" steeped in
body fluids and beseeching

  passers-by to become a
source for them of more. You didn't
   in the seventies visit
New York without alighting here.

  Except for the time I played
grease monkey to a line of fists,
   overseeing their pin-lit
point of departure, it's not so

      much misbehaving as mis-
beholding at the Mineshaft I
      recall: the pleasures—and pains—
it accorded were visual

      ones largely, testament as
much to the limits of desire
      as to its promptings, if it
was desire I witnessed and not

      Shock Theater. **WHEN YOU DREAMED
OF MOVING TO MANHATTAN, THIS
      WAS WHERE YOU MEANT—BUT WISDOM—
FEAR?—INTERVENED AND YOU DID NOT.**

Hot spots 6/ The Continental Baths

    Miss M wasn't the only
"divinity" breaching the walls
       of New York's Continental
Baths in its '70s heyday.

    After taking a few hits
off a reefer proffered by one
       of its administering
angels, I "saw" that so long as

    men kept drifting together
and apart from each other, as
       they were doing here and as
Michael and I were doing,

    we would always be *theirs*—our
mothers working in compliance
       with the dictates of a Great
Mother (I had been reading Jung),

    in the interests of whose
revolutionary defeat
       of Patriarchy we were
enrolled. Then thanks to a bathhouse

    attendant who lent the rear
door of his holy of holies
       to the fond ministrations
of my tongue, I slowly "came down."

> *An avenging angel he*
> *must have been who gave you the case*
> *of hepatitis you brought*
> *home.* **WHICH, IN THE DEPLOYMENT OF**
>
> **NURSING SKILLS HONED DURING THE**
> **WAR IN NAM, OCCASIONED SOME OF**
> **MICHAEL'S FINEST HOURS WITH YOU**
> **AND SOME OF YOURS, POEMS POURING**
>
> **FROM YOU WITH THEIR EVIDENCE**
> **OF WHAT YOU HAD JUST "DETECTED":**
> **IN THE TAINTED PRECINCTS OF**
> **GAY MALE LIFE "WOMEN" EVERYWHERE.**

Hot spots 7/ San Francisco

    Four late summer visits in
as many years saw you returned
        to that Sodom by the Sea,
that Golden-Gated Gomorrah

    of your imagination.
Even mornings at Lafayette
        Park would find you at work on
the "garb" of your investiture:

    a fabulous tan. Evenings,
after dinner with your friend and
        host George T, you became an
attendant in proximity

    to one or more of the "teats" —
in the baths, glory hole and corn
        hole clubs — by means of which She
was granting you access to Her.

    All the while of course it was
Her tentacles that were taking
        hold of you. The first time I
disengaged myself from Her was

    at an afternoon preview
of a Mission Hill orgy site
        at which given pride of place
was a hospital table which

would be made available,
I was told, "for surgical sex."
Would they be extremities
of *Hers*—or of mine—that would be

making it to the block, I
wondered. Before I boarded a
plane back to Boston that last
time, my parting shot to George was,

"How can you *live* like this?"—**WHEN,
AMONG GEORGE AND HIS FRIENDS, FOR WHOM
YOUR WORDS WERE SOMETHING OF A
JOKE—IT WAS ONLY *YOU* WHO HAD!**

Hot spots 8/ Boston Tubs, et al.

       There the clubs lay, all across
America, posing questions
         I had only within them
entertained answers for—about

       how many times someone could
be punched in the testicles, say,
         before he cried "uncle" (as
many apparently as I

       liked, in New Orleans); how long
I could endure a choke hold (not
         very long, in Miami);
and what I could feel comfortable

       being called, in New York, in
the sack. *I was surprised at how*
         intense sex became for me
when someone appended to his

       imperatives ("suck this," "eat
that") the word "faggot"—an address
         that fell upon eager ears
in Boston—like manna from hell.

       So this was what "Pride" had brought
you to—the aerobics of self-
         loathing, and its diction! Which
worked to my advantage so long

as the roles adopted were
clear and well-maintained: when I asked
someone kneeling I had been
calling "faggot," to stand up, let

me drop to *mine* and have him
call me one *too*, he slinked away.
**ALAS, YOU HAD UNDERSCORED
THE EVENT'S ARBITRARINESS—**

**YOUR TAKING TURNS USING THE
WORD "FAGGOT" WOULD HAVE MADE FOR TOO
PLAIN AN ACKNOWLEDGMENT THAT
THERE WERE NO "REAL MEN" IN THE ROOM.**

Hot spots 9/ Instructions to "my boy"

      I'm "the daddy"; you, "my boy."
Just back from your school team's winning
      the game, you strip down to your
sweaty underwear, hit the bed,

      and, feigning sleep, close your eyes.
Coming upon you "by surprise,"
      I undress myself and start
licking the sweat off you, toe to

      head, saving for the end the
"dirty places"—pits, crotch and ass—
      and after a while express
the fear that you might wake up to

      find your dick in daddy's mouth—
which is your signal. You "waken,
      aghast" at what you see: "What
the fuck is with you, dad, are you

      a queer or something?" you ask.
You attempt to push me away
      without really ceasing to
have sex with me, until you "find"

      that you like what you're feeling.
Your shoving stops, especially
      after I tell you—and you
pretend to swallow the notion—

>   that all boys do this for their
> dads, they just don't talk about
>   it with each other; then I
> Claim that you provide better head
>
>   than can be obtained elsewhere
> at home. *In the long governance*
>   *between boys and dads, what bonds—*
> *banns!—do you not here dishonor?*
>
>   **THE SWEET, HOMOEROTIC**
> **YEARNING HERE ENCODED CONCERNS**
>   **A BOY'S LOVE FOR HIS FATHER**
> **WHICH IS NOT, BY A MOTHER, BLOCKED.**

Program 1/ My (first?) bottom
—December 31, 1982

      Forty—and still meeting men
in bars whose stories—delivered
      in a wash of alcohol
and received that way—it was thought

      I should remember. Brilliant—
in the course of my bicycle
      toolings about town, coming
upon the greeting of faces

      I knew I knew with *my* high
five, the generic "Hi, Guy!" There
      was a pattern: friends I thought
were mine were distancing themselves

      from me: Johnie B, who sent
a note disclaiming our friendship:
      no reason given; Larry
B, who read me the riot act

      on my "condescending" bar
behavior. Well, to pass New Year's
      Eve, at least there was Randy
M. Nope! He would be rounding off

      a dinner foursome I'd not
been asked to join. The night found me
      at Sporter's gay bar downing
martinis in the company

  of Pat S, more fan than friend,
more tipsy collaborator
  than either. *You'd exhausted
Boston—or it had you. New York*

  *promised a deepening of
intimacy with family
  and the lit crowd—and more sex
than you were managing to have*

  *here. Yet every effort made
to get you off (a drafted P
  and S away) availed you
nothing.* **JUST MAY HAVE SAVED YOUR LIFE**.

Program 2/ January 1, 1983

  On what I thought was a whim
and not what it seemed thereafter,
   the last conveyance leaving
my station, I decided I

  wouldn't drink on New Year's Day,
curious to see if doing
   without booze would have any
effect on me. Did it ever!

  I went from being someone
whose walls and ceilings were coming
   down around him to angel
of the house—in one day getting

  my drawers in order. That night
found me at Skipper's, a ginger
   ale in my hands, mourning a
self who had lost the power not

  to spend every night of the
week in a bar—which I sensed I
   would now be able to claim.
Day three: you'd "forgotten how to

  walk" and "are losing your mind."
No, back rub offered by my date
   for Symphony doesn't help.
A call to Herbert M, a friend

>   and alcoholic who was
> likely to know what even non-
>   alcoholics like myself
> go through when they stop drinking. No
>
>   answer: break date; take myself
> to meeting I brought John V to
>   months ago. *Now there was your
> alkie, nightly knocking himself*
>
>   *out with six-packs.* **JOHN, WHO MAY
> HAVE NEEDED IT, NEVER RETURNED;
>   YOU, WHO MUST HAVE FOUND SOMETHING
> YOU WANTED FROM IT, GOT ON BOARD.**

Program 3/ First boondoggle

      Deciding that I *wouldn't*—
not that I *couldn't* in safety—
      drink, I declared myself a
member of the Arlington Street

      circle of love and was met
by resistance from one of its
      members. "I'm having trouble
with the newcomer denial

      about their alcoholism":
thus spake *Shawn J*, who seemed by
      articulateness to "take
possession" of the meeting. "You

      thought I was alluding to
you by my comments?!" he told me.
      "That's how self-centered you are!"
Ten years later I asked Shawn if,

      having gotten off to a
bad start, we might now become friends.
      His reply: "Maybe in the
next life." The next life must not have

      looked far away—he was near
death by then, having believed, as
      he averred at meetings, that
"God hadn't gotten [him] sober

>	to give [him] AIDS"—that is, that
codes of safer sex behavior
>		didn't apply to him. *The
circles of love have proved themselves*

>	*often enough circles of
detestation—face it, haven't
>		you stayed sober to spite Shawn
J, who expected you to drink,*

>	*not because you were convinced
you were an alcoholic? Now
>		that Shawn's gone...* **TALK ABOUT YOUR
CASE—YOUR *CASES*—OF DENIAL!**

Program 4/ I can see clearly now

   The purple foyer walls were
a mess of peelings, the result
   of my having painted them
years ago without a primer;

   the bathroom ceiling had a
hole in it big enough to drop
   a body through—my hiring
Rodney B for renovations

   was part of the same New Year's
resolutions that led me to
   stop drinking. By day nine, my
inner walls and ceiling had come

   down too—as approaching the
church basement blackboard, chalk in hand—
   I said to the group, "I had
always thought myself a success,

   having transcended (the line
climbed off the board) the bourgeois needs
   of work and love. Now my life's
line seems to have started well, then

   plunged into the shitter." Sad
parabola. The last pieces
   of furniture you bought for
your Revere Street digs—a super

>refrigerator (you ate
out) and a tea table (never
>touched the stuff), what needs did they
answer to but for round-the-clock

>ice cubes and gallons of gin?
"Look at yourself": is this what he
>meant, the friend of Tommy S
at Sporter's you turned down and who

>then took your inventory?
YOU LOOKED AND THERE YOU WERE, A
>**MAN WITH A PH.D. WHO'D**
BECOME SOMEONE'S BOOZY DOORMAN.

Program 5/ Second boondoggle

If you admitted you were
an alcoholic in pursuit
    of recovery, you had
to go to meetings for the rest

    of your life, so that you could,
what? in hewing to "the Steps"
    lose everything that made you
you? You knew of drunken poets-

    did you know any who had
gotten sober? That's where a trip
    I made, ninety days sober,
came in handy. At meetings in

    the Village, I heard poets,
novelists, actors speak about
    being sober and going
on with their art: I wouldn't have

    to sacrifice a self to
"the program" to have it work for
    me: what was left but for me
to surrender to it, which came

    about during a Broadway
theater production of "Cats,"
    in which Grizabella—and
wasn't I as bedraggled from

   years of head-banging about
the bushes as she?—is conveyed
    up into the Other Side
layer: she would get a new life,

   a fresh start. I wanted one
too, and through eyes veiled by tears—or
    with a mind focused by them—
I saw only one way for me

   to get it: to go back to
Boston and assert I had a
    disease. **YOUR FINEST HOUR—AND**
IN YOUR LIFE (THANK YOU, THANK YOU) MINE.

Program 6/ Into the light
—for Paul Schmidt (1934-'99)

When Paul Schmidt asked, the last time
you saw him alive in Cambridge,
if he might sleep sometime in
your new digs, you murmured "Maybe"—

after all he did for you!—
snatching you—back from Paris in
'66 and eager to
demonstrate competency, new

to you, in Greek—from out the
Esplanade's caressing darks and
into light. Literary
lights they were at a dinner at

which you feasted on Lamb, Charles
Lamb's "Dissertation upon Roast
Pig" being, at one point, on
the discussion menu, as what,

at others, was not—in his
townhouse, with a library! on
Dartmouth Street. Brightest among
those gathered lights was Richard H,

whom you would be privileged
to take for the next fifteen years
as your friend and mentor. "Yes,
but I gave as well as I got!

In the copy he inscribed
to me of his own translation
of Rimbaud, for having brought
him in '83, just three months

sober myself, to his first
A.A. meeting and the first day
of what would translate into
fifteen years of sobriety

and numerous luminous
translations. **PAUL CREDITS YOU WITH
HAVING GOT HIM OUT OF [HIS]
OWN "SEASON IN HELL."** *This is yours.*

Program 7/ Lovers and a friend

      Before Craig, Eddie, Maxim,
there was drink, a fifth of liqueur
      loosening my trousers the
first time I had sex with a man.

      How else did I envision
the career of teaching, to which
      I aspired, but as one long
faculty party over which

      martinis presided—a
vision Albee's "Virginia Woolf"
      uncomfortably confirmed?
And liquor helped negotiate

      the claims of my college (frat)
and my early gay (bar) lives, those
      irreconcilables then.
Later, when the lovers, the jobs,

      and the possibilities
of moving out of (or even
      within) Boston seemed to have
vanished, the drink stood at my side.

      Suddenly, before you had
proved whether or not you could not
      drink, you cut it, on a whim,
out. Was that any way to treat

> a lover or a friend? Time
passed and then... a chance encounter
> in a restaurant, where you
asked for non-alcoholic beer
>
> and drank half of it before
you realized—ah, that blessed
> relief—that you were with your
old friend. And you put the bottle
>
> down, proving, of course, that you
could have just one drink and put the
> bottle down. **YOU CAN ALSO
GO ONE MORE DAY WITHOUT A DRINK.**

Program 8/ Adding a program

      I'd gone six months without a
drink and there I was, again, crammed
        into half of two closets,
one "confessional" opening

      into the other (or closed
off by it), recapping my "sins"
        to a man I didn't know
who, from his vial of poppers,

      offered me hits, incense of
which I did not partake—unless
        being in such close quarters—
so pervasive was the stench of

      "Amy" in them—amounted
itself, in a program I was
        already working, to a
slip. *Reflect on how you spent your*

      first night free of alcohol,
on your knees, taking dictation
        in Combat Zone "offices"
that are all gone now, as "acting

      out" behavior on your part
was not, having anonymous
        sex being important to
retain as an option, you thought,

*now that drinking was not. You
only hadn't drunk too much in
  the dawning of your Love Quests
so as not to blunt your late night*

* skills in giving pleasure and
receiving it. Another sort
  of soberness? Another
band of flagellants! But is it*

* in your interest really
to have no way left of acting
  out?* **YOU'LL BE SURPRISED AT WHAT CAN BE DONE WHEN YOU ASK FOR HELP.**

Program 9/ Too little, too much

      An abusive father of
four; a married bisexual
         who wanted to cut the dyke
out of herself; Sis G, a dyke

      scared by her history of
S/M; and Saul S, whose "bottom
         line" included not locking
eyes with anyone for longer

      than three seconds—regimen
of his which I sought at meetings
         to demolish with my hard
stares, so delightful a country

      did immersion in those dark
pools portend; Julio; Pauline;
         the two Mindys—"Fuck" or "No
Fuck," according to whether she

      was able to curse or not;
and I, married to convenience,
         not a man: what we trusted
the meetings and their aftermaths

      to supply us with was safe
passage, first, through Saturday night,
         by means of one vast dinner
spread on Beacon Hill and a film...

        and then through life. *What did Saul*
of the Deflected Eyes later
        see in his mirror but a
pierced and tattooed Los Angeles

        bar back—and the cynosure
of all eyes! And Sis? She cried up
        a meeting for sexual
anorectics, so far had her

        pendulum gotten away
from her. **YOU LITTLE KNOW WHERE THAT**
        PENDULUM WILL TAKE YOU ONCE
YOU SET YOUR SIGHTS ON SWINGING "FREE."

Love 1/ Nay-saying

     Icy and blue Paul M's lips
would turn in the heat of passion.
       Or, when he was in my arms,
did the chill indicate his not

     responding to me? Noting
his cooling down after only
       a week of what I'd defined
as the beginning of a new

     relationship, I asked him
if he liked having sex with me.
       "Yes," he said, "only not so
often." "Every *other* day?" "No."

     "Once a week?" "No." "A month?" "No."
(Having boarded it, I didn't
       know where this train would drop me off.)
"Once every two months?" Bingo, that

     was it. To the idea of
a relationship with him I
       then said "No." You *said No? Paul
had said it for both of you, no?*

     *although saying No to you
might have amounted to saying
       Yes to some situation
of his own devising, moving*

>   *to L.A., for instance.* There
> was another instance the guy
>   in a bar whose lover was
> out of town. That might have worked if
>
>   I'd had a lover of my
> *own* to cheat on. But sex with him
>   wouldn't have got me that. So...
> **NO. IF YOU SAID IT ENOUGH TIMES**
>
> **MAYBE THE WAY MIGHT BE MADE
> CLEAR TO SAYING YES. EVEN THE
>   GOOD, YOU REMINDED YOURSELF,
> WAS AN ENEMY OF THE BEST.**

Love 2/ Seeing clearly now

      The sun was out, turning the
curly blond wires-hair—on Sterling
      G's legs to gold, as he slipped
down beside my blanket on the

      Charles River Esplanade—the
first time he and I met—prelude
      to an evening's taking of
pleasure. The experience was

      now and again repeated,
but why, when there were so many
      apples on the tree, eat of
one only? So came ten years of

      "splendid isolation," which
only peeled back after the booze
      was put down along with my
habit of permitting people

      into my life who were good
for one night of love only. Then
      my eyes snapped open—or was
that a gate slamming shut?—and what

      had been kept from me—the world's
pain and suffering and my own—
      I saw. Sterling had his own
pains to endure (his mother's death,

    the break with Dino). Might a
bond with each other equip us
       both in the creation of
what Ralph H calls "another kind

       of paradise"? *Your powers*
of attracting men to yourself
       had vanished, AIDS was rampant,
so you surrendered to martial —

       uh — marital bliss. **WHICH COMES,**
AS YOUR FRIEND EDWARD F SAYS, OF
       FINDING ONE'S PARTNER CAN BE
GOOD FOR MORE THAN ONE THING ONLY.

Love 3/ The arrivistes

  By his tall, fair "other son,"
as your father calls Sterling G,
  he may be reminded of
his beloved, older brother

  (the Sturmbannführer Jöse)
lost in World War II. Certainly
  Sterling calls to mind the blond
prince who sets his cap for—no, his

  crown on—the servant girl—her-
self!-in any of the well-thumbed
  Deutschen Romanzen women
in your mother's circle exchanged

  among themselves. And then there's
you, who, except for when it comes
  to telling jokes, thinks himself
free of prejudice. To be sure,

  I wanted out of Queens—in
which, as a member of the bridge
  and tunnel crowd, I didn't
know a soul without an ethnic

  name—whereas the man I met
on the steps of Perkins Hall at
  Harvard, which my parents had
Bought—uh, brought—me to, introduced

himself as a Roosevelt!
In Boston, my new friends had names
   like Hunt, Smith, Truslow, Ward, so
I was finally storming an

   invisible barricade.
After a few "divorces," in
   which my ethnicity might
have somehow played a part, I got

   myself partnered with Sterling—
WHO EMBODIES THE "AUTHENTIC
   AMERICAN" YOU'VE LONGED TO
CAST YOUR "IMMIGRANT SLIME" BEFORE.

Love 4/ Appearances revealing

     "What did you do, dress in the
dark?" The query leapt from the mouth
         of then office manager
at my job, Penelope N.

     I looked down at my long-sleeved
white shirt, black pants, before they had
         become de rigueur: Why was
I dressed for Dullsville? And why else

     was I letting myself pile
on the pounds, but that I hadn't
         given a thought to how I
appeared in the South End, amply

     provided with mirroring
correctives to my self-regard.
         The dark? That was where your four
years of monogamy had brought

     you to: four years of time served.
You biked to Cambridge to enact
         a scenario you had
spelled out over the phone to one

     Tom C, in which "a boy" wakes
to find "his father" licking him—...
         On my return jag, I ran
into Jerry R. outside of

Grolier's, who asked, what had I
been doing? Then before I had
a chance of answering him:
"Whatever it is, keep doing

it," he added, "you look great!"
THAT SETTLED IT. OPENING A
TWOSOME UP MIGHT, LIKE WALKING
A DOG, LEAD TO MORE FRIENDS FOR BOTH

YOU *AND* STERLING. TAKE NOTICE
OF STERLING'S WARNING, THOUGH: "UNSTUFF
THAT BAG OF WINDS AND IT WILL
NOT EASILY BE SHUT AGAIN."

Love 5/ Le mot juste

      Were we releasing a bag
of winds, a barn door we might not
         be able to close again?
Since "the opening up of our

      relationship" after four
years (he after five) meant each of
         us would be "sleeping around
for the two of us," Sterling came

      up with a contract which man-
dated (on our dates with men
         other than ourselves) no fucking, no
sucking without a condom, no

      deep kissing even! and no
seeing anyone more than three
         times—no "real sex," he might have
ordered. It wasn't long before

      we'd each violated
the contract, as we each confessed—
         and were absolved. *After a*
token cessation required for

      focus' sake, you reverted
to type—to stereotype—of
         the homosexual not
able to stay "faithful" to his

  partner. Helping us maintain
our contract would be place—Boston—
  and time—the '90s—during
the watch of a "no fun" Mayor

  who saw Boston's one "dirty
movie house" and one gay bathhouse
  disappear. **WHEN SOMEONE
ASKED—AT ONE OF TIM W'S**

  **JULY 4TH PARTIES—WHETHER
YOU AND I WERE MONOGAMOUS,
  STERLING DELIGHTED WITH THE
NIGHT'S MOT JUSTE: "WE'RE MONOGAMISH."**

Love 6/ Practicing what I preach

       Upon catching his wife or
girlfriend in bed with another
         man, what does a straight man do
but take a knife or a gun to

       the two of them?—the subject
of how many movies and much
         TV and print news—whereas
the appropriate response of

       gay males' finding their lovers
in bed with someone else—if they
         don't actually join the
couple in question—would be to

       sequester themselves stage right
or left and masturbate to the...
         footage before their eyes, as
in "Taxi Zum Klo" the lover

       does, life having turned for once
into pornography. *When your
         chance came to do precisely
that, having found Sterling at the*

       *baths, after you'd each told the
other you were going to work
         out at your respective gyms,
you burst into tears and stumbled*

home! WHOEVER SAID YOURS WOULD
BE AN EASY HALL TO PAD? HERE
    IS THE RULE OF THUMB I WOULD
IMPRESS YOU WITH: "IF A PARTNER

    CAN'T BE MONOGAMOUS IN
A RELATIONSHIP'S GETTING-TO-
    KNOW-YOU PHASE, HE CAN'T BE SAID
TO DESERVE A LOVER; IF ONE

    PARTNER AFTER A TIME CAN'T
RELEASE THE OTHER FROM THE RULE
    OF MONOGAMY, HE MAY
NOT DESERVE TO *KEEP* A LOVER."

Love 7/ "I just want to be with you"

       Those were they, the seven (last!)
words, a kind of mantra of (co-)
       dependency which have spelled
doom to the partnerships I have

       been involved in over the
years—had I picked partners in fact
       for the likelihood of their
eventually uttering

       them?—except that for this once—
my karma coming back to haunt
       me?—I was uttering them
to Sterling—or I as much as

       uttered them at the end of
a fifth weekend in a row he'd
       spent in Provincetown without
me. Beckoned back to Boston by

       rumors of my distraction,
Sterling was distraught that upon
       meeting me at the dock I
wasn't *more* distraught. Why else had

       he agreed to cut short his
weekend? *Of course this was the mash
       note to your mother that your
staying home (with her) sick from St.*

> *Anne's Prep was uttering for*
> *you and that her notes about your*
> > *being sick were uttering*
> *in turn.* **THE INDICATION THAT**
>
> > **YOU HAVE BEEN FOR ONCE LUCKY—**
> **OR HEALTHY—IN LOVE FINDS SUPPORT**
> > **IN STERLING'S INDEPENDENCE,**
> **IN HIS FAILING, PRECISELY, TO**
>
> > **UTTER THOSE WORDS, MARKING HIM**
> **AS SOMEONE FOR WHOM LOVE EXISTS**
> > **FREE OF POSSESSIVENESS. CAN**
> **YOU GET ON THE SAME PAGE WITH HIM?**

Love 8/ Sense and sensibility

      Sterling's mother, who died a
month before he and I took up
      with each other, I never
met, although he assures me she

      would have loved me: a person
who cries easily—as I did,
      for instance, in the Christmas
gift exchange at which Kim gave me

      a copy of the wedding
photo of her marriage to Marc
      in which the immediate
family members, six of them,

      hold hands with their respective
partners (and just as much part of
      the family, holding hands,
are her brother Sterling and I).

      You are such a cry baby
that Sterling doesn't see a film
      with you without bringing a
hanky you will in the night be

      needing. The gifts Sterling makes
to his four nieces come Christmas
      are practical ones—cash—which
Rudl, my father, has bestowed

>annually on his wife
and children for as far back as
>I can remember. But no
one seems to enjoy shopping more

>than Sterling's father, each year
adding to my World War II stash
>of collectibles—a gift
he's as sentimental about

>as I am. **SO NO WONDER
EACH FATHER CAN CLAIM, AS HE DOES
>TO HIS SON'S PARTNER, "YOU'RE LIKE
ANOTHER SON (READ: SELF) TO ME."**

Love 9/ Ports of call

      Sterling managed, on his first
day in Guatemala, to hike
        to and climb up a bubbling
volcano, Pacaya, something

      his Antiguan hosts, David
O and Tony S, have never
        done. He was a lover of
swimming, skiing, and canoeing

      when I met him; in the last
few years, he's added sailing to
        his activities roster;
now thoughts of hot air balloons dance

      in his head. My construction
of his vacation ideal: a
        balloon ride over a live
volcano in Iceland! Meetings

      with a behavioralist
before our day trip to Lowell
        (my "gateway to the world," he
dubbed it) has led to sojourns in

      Salem, Portsmouth, Provincetown —
also San Francisco, London
        and Paris. Where is it now
I'm afraid to go? *"Nowhere so*

long as Sterling goes with you!",
piped up Dr. D, your script source-
      WHICH IGNORES ALL THE PROGRESS
YOU'VE MADE IN OVERCOMING YOUR

      TRAVEL PHOBIA! USE THE
TOOLS—PATIENCE, PRESCRIPTION DRUGS AND
      THE ASKING OF A HIGHER
POWER FOR HELP—THAT HELPED YOU IN

      LOWELL. NOTICE, TOO, HOW FORT
LAUDERDALE, MONTREAL BECKON—
      WITH THEIR PROMISE OF COMFORTS
FOR THE OLDER GAY MAN ALONE.

Miscellany iii/ Marco

      Swarthy, lustrous, and beyond
beautiful—a diamond of
      the first water in the rough,
so to speak, a few days' growth of

      beard upon his angel's face,
he appears before me in the
      locker room of M's gym with
an erection that, inasmuch

      as we are alone, I have
to think I am occasioning.
      Unless the occasion is.
He notices me noticing

      and introduces himself.
Would he like to play sometime? Yes,
      but we're both busy that night.
"Call on the weekend," I implore.

      Then, to sweeten, as it were,
the pot, I offer him a tall,
      handsome, blond forty-year-old
who I know would like to play with

      us as well. *"Not old enough,"*
he mumbles—*he wants me alone."*
      Or to suffer the ordeal
of having only one older

man at a time pawing him.
At fifty-seven, can I be
his type? What you offer can
appeal—service and a stud fee.

He's moving Saturday to
Canton, his rent having gotten
so steep. "Do you want money?"
I ask. He demurs—too faintly.

I'm relieved: our connection's
finally making sense. **ALTHOUGH YOUR NEED TO BESTOW CASH ON HIM MAY EXCEED HIS NEED TO HAVE IT.**

Miscellany iv: . . . Polo

    I spell the role out for him:
a "sleeping son's" being wakened
        at long last by his "father's"
lips. He seems compliant. To the

        undressing room. "Lights come up"
on Marco, nude, awake, playing
        with himself athwart a day
bed, my scenario (my sex

        extender) apparently
tossed aside, signaling only
        (now we're deep into his script)
that he wants it hot, hard and now.

    His wishes, in the desired
short order, fulfilled, there are two
        things Marco asks before he
bolts; one, "You won't tell anyone

        about this, will you? I have
a lover." Well, who doesn't! But
        okay. "Oh, and that CD
player on your desk—how do you

        like it?" "Fine." "Because I want
to get one just like it." I whisk
        the big bill out I keep at
hand for just such an occasion,

  and—pressing it to his palm—
say, "For the CD player." *So
  you're not paying for sex, and
he's not a hustler—just daddy's*

  *boy (after all!) asking for
something he "needs."* **LOOK, HE'S PLAINLY
  ONE OF THE GREAT BEAUTIES AT
YOUR GYM, THE ONLY DOWNSIDE TO**

  **FAMILIARITY WITH
WHOM IS NOT THE MONEY HE MAY
  COST YOU BUT THAT HE'S ENJOINED
YOU TO SECRECY ABOUT HIM.**

Miscellany v/ Todd

 "Always when you're around the tall blond boys you crave
you become another person."—Robert H

 Redheads, he might have added,
of which in Boston he figures
 as a shining example.
And brunettes. And boys with black hair.

 And why should boys have to be
tall for me to worship the ground
 upon which they walk, or the
pool table, say, in Paradise

 on Thursday of last week, when
the best-looking stripper I have
 ever seen on stage go-goed
his way into my heart, or some

 other arm? Afterwards,
collecting on the debt to him
 his beauty had put us in,
and distributing among us

 other favors—permitted
pats and intimate touches of
 that holy of holies—his
private parts: did he, I whispered,

 do private shows? No, he said.
Talk of the Golden Gate's being
 shut in one's face. If only
I'd followed that query up with

   mention of a specific—
and substantial—sum in exchange
   for his willingness to sit
on my face... Adding insult to

   injury! And would that have
addressed your chief complaint—being
   gay and turning old and gray?
PROMPTINGS OF BEAUTY INTO SELF—

   DISCOVERY CAN ALWAYS
BE PROFANE IN ORIGIN. START,
   IF YOU WILL, ON... A BOTTOM
AND WORK YOUR WAY UP TO A TOP.

Miscellany vi/ Construction sites

      In the course of emptying
your shelves, so you could position
      yourself before the classic
column in what now constitutes

      your Robert Giard portrait
of '87, you found out
      that your books were infected
with worms. They've infiltrated you

      too, of course, your classic good
looks (what else was the column meant
      to suggest?) having come clean
away, gravity having pulled

      that crisp construction project,
your face, down into the dust. Now
      the only mirror you can
bear to see yourself in is the

      one suspended over your
dentist Dr. Varnerin's chair,
      in which the folds that were once your
cheeks hang not down but off to the

      side. I may not be my own
type, but that doesn't mean I can't
      be someone else's. Stefan,
rolling onto me the project

   he had been subsidizing
by the hour, that of his young face
    and lovely body, recently
opined—of course I was again

   on my back, and he could peer
between my folds—as to how "the
    eyes were the windows of the
soul" and that, he realized, my

   "eyes were beautiful." FROM THE
MOUTH... OF A BABE! *And how much were*
    you paying Stefan an hour
to comment on Your Loveliness?

Miscellany vii/ Mother's funeral

    Urging family and friends
at the Ridgewood funeral door
        to view the open casket
and testify with him to the

        fact that "she's not dead," his wife;
"look, she's only sleeping"—the woes
        of my father extended
to his running from car to car

        in the cortege asking "Where's
Sterling?", my partner of sixteen
        years, because he belonged at
my side in the first limousine,

        until my father found him
down the line, happily paired with
        his bosom buddy du jour,
Helga K. And with whom, when he

        had a mind to, would he not
unload his bosom to? Even
        my mother's brother, Joe T—
whose house, after he'd taunted me

        for belonging in Greenwich
Village, I vowed never again
        to enter—let me know how
much he and everybody liked

Sterling, "for being able
to talk about anything with
anybody." *The Gay Lib
jubilance du jour: should it have*

preventing you from mourning

*prevented you from mourning
your "first girlfriend"—and last?!* ANON.
ATTENTION WAS THEN DUE THE
GUARDIAN OF THE SOLITUDE

WITHDRAWAL FROM CONTINENCE,
MEMORY AND RECOGNITION
EVEN HAD THRUST UPON HER:
HER HERO AND YOURS, YOUR FATHER.

Miscellany viii/ Amour fou

      Tall and fair (and nothing like
her short dark keg of a husband)
        I came along bringing to
mind her father, dead of TB,

      my vulnerability
taking the form of a full range
        of childhood diseases—mumps,
measles, chicken pox, and time and

      again the need of a note
getting me out of gym class and
        under her care (in her arms?)
at home. "Your mother did something

      to you," claims your therapist
Chris, with whom you've been discussing
        your "case" for something like a
decade now; that something came to

      be described in a workshop
you attended for forty-six
        weeks as "emotional in-
cest," in which the two of you might

      have been complicit. *Surely*
the competition must have seemed
        like one between the German
prince of my mother's fancy and...

>   *this gnome. But no, not really.*
> *Your father's steel fabrication*
> >   *company and the money*
> *that came thereof trumping every*
>
> >   *time your "edjumication,"*
> *his pejorative coinage for*
> >   *your college success — your forte —*
> *propped up by his blue-collar one.*
>
> > **ATTENDED BY YOUR FATHER**
> > **FOR THE LAST SIX YEARS OF HER LIFE,**
> > >   **NEVER HAD YOUR MOTHER'S CHOICE**
> > **SEEMED MORE SENSIBLE, MORE PROFOUND.**

Miscellany ix/ Old

      Twenty years ago Harry
K wanted to leave Sporter's bar
      with you—just go out the door,
not go home—and you turned him down,

      for fear that the bar, that nest
of eyes, might think that in him, a
      portly older man, you had
found your level. What goes around

      comes around. It's now ten years
since a derelict shambling by
      you on Tremont Street looked up
and murmured, good-naturedly,

      "Hi ya, Pops!" Veritas in
vino, indeed—for all that you
      might argue, in this instance,
that the mirror was a cracked and

      misted one. Remember that
college caricature of you
      in relation to which there
was much to learn, much to accept.

      Fact is, you're suffering from
an illness you share with all of
      nature and for which there is
no cure yet: the aging process.

>   *What I miss most is turning*
> *my head after a handsome boy*
> >   *or man on the street — rubber*
> *necking — to find he had turned too,*
>
> >   *in my direction. After*
> *which... No more of that, Pops! You will*
> >   *find yourself become a blind*
> *spot, a blip on the horizon —*
>
> >   *invisible — or sneered*
> *at, treated as if aging were*
> >   *a moral fault. Isn't it?*
> *Have done with it.* **ALL IN GOOD TIME.**

About the Author

I credit William McBrien with steering me away from Business and into Literature—at a college that was not St. Anne's and where Remo Iannucci, my first mentor, taught German.

Richard Howard, whom I met through Paul Schmidt, published poems of mine in American Review 18 and New American Review 11. (A friend called me excitedly to report that he'd seen a poem of mine on a Venezuelan bookstand. My chest, not to mention my head, swelled.)

I was an instigator and editor, along with Walta Borawski, Sal Farinella, Charley Shively, David Eberly, and Michael Bronski, of the Boston Gay review. We were so filled with contradictory urges, I'm surprised we got through one editorial meeting, let alone eight.

I worked on a first chapbook of mine, called "Shaping Possibilities" (1980), for populist Peter Payack's Imaginary Press. My first "big" book was "Lasting Relations" (1984) with the effervescent Felice Picano. A second was "Long Division" (1993) with Writers Block Publishing Co. and Kevin Sharpe.

Louisa Salerno's been a pal; my twice having been asked to be a judge for her Grolier Poetry Prize (which I won once) gave me the courage to take on an anthology, "Gents, Bad Boys & Barbarians: New Gay Male Poetry," for Sasha Alyson (1995) of Alyson Publications.

By the time I followed "Gents" with a second selection, "This New Breed" (2004), my poetry had found a spiritual home in Orchard House Press, from which has emerged—along with reprintings of "Lasting Relations" (1980) and "Long Division" (1993)—"Period Pieces" (1997), "Gottscheers" (1997), and "Talks in the Blue" (2009).